BEGINNING MOBILES

PEGGY PARISH

BEGINNING MOBILES

ILLUSTRATED BY LYNN SWEAT

Macmillan Publishing Co., Inc., New York
Collier Macmillan Publishers, London

For Phyllis,

who loves to edit craft books,

with love

Macmillan Publishing Co., Inc.
866 Third Avenue, New York, N.Y. 10022
Collier Macmillan Canada Ltd.
Printed in the United States of America

10 9 8 7 6 5 4 3 2 1

LIBRARY OF CONGRESS CATALOGING IN PUBLICATION DATA

Parish, Peggy
  Beginning mobiles.

  (A Ready-to-read handbook)
  SUMMARY: Demonstrates how to make simple mobiles from
household materials.
  1. Mobiles (Sculpture)—Juvenile literature.
[1. Mobiles (Sculpture)   2. Handicraft]   I. Sweat,
Lynn.   II. Title.
TT899.P37   731'.55   79-9950   ISBN 0-02-770030-5

CONTENTS

Things to Remember   7

How to Make Egg Cup Forms   8

How to Make a Frame   9

Flower Pots   10

Fish   12

Merry-Go-Round   13

Jack-O'-Lanterns   14

Witches   16

Skeletons and Ghosts   19

Turkeys   22

Christmas Stockings   24

Candles   26

Christmas Trees   28

Curly Ques   31

Yarn Jumbles   32

Snowmen	34
Hearts	36
Baskets	38
Bunnies	40
May Pole	42
Monkeys	45
Cradles	47
Straw Bursts	49
Clowns	51
Bugs	54
Popcorn	57
Pictures	58
Lanterns	60
Butterflies	62

THINGS TO REMEMBER

1. Read the whole project before you begin.

2. Find the materials needed before you start to work.

3. Work on old newspaper.

4. Use poster paints.

5. Use a good *all-purpose* glue.

6. Let things dry on wax paper or plastic wrap so they won't stick.

7. Clean and put things away when you finish working.

8. *Try out your own ideas!*

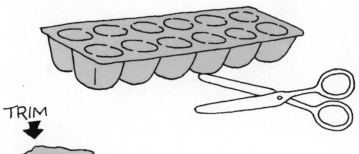

TRIM

HOW TO MAKE EGG CUP FORMS

1. Use cardboard egg cartons.

2. Cut the egg cup sections apart.

GLUE

3. Trim the edges to make them even.

4. Glue two egg cups together. They may not fit perfectly, but that doesn't matter.

5. Let the glue dry.

STRIP OF OAK TAG PAPER

HOW TO MAKE A FRAME

1. Cut a strip of oak tag or cardboard as wide and as long as a yardstick.

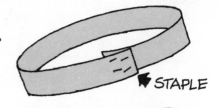

STAPLE

2. Bend it to make a circle. Staple in place.

3. Punch four holes as shown.

PUNCH HOLES

4. Cut two pieces of string of equal length.

5. Put each string through the holes as shown. Tie the ends together.

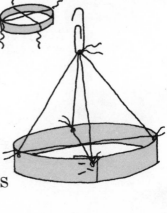

6. Bend a paper clip as shown. Put it through the top strings to make a hook for hanging.

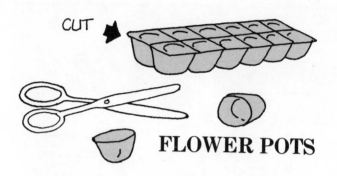

FLOWER POTS

1. Make a frame (page 9).

2. Cut the sections of an egg carton apart. Trim the tops of the egg cups to make them even.

3. Cut the egg cups to look like flowers. Paint them if you wish.

4. For stems, paint pipe cleaners.

5. Cut leaves from art or crepe paper. Glue them to the stems.

6. Glue a stem to each flower. Let the glue dry.

7. For pots, use small paper cups. Glue a piece of cardboard to the top of each cup. Let the glue dry.

8. Cut the cardboard to fit. Paint the pots if you wish.

9. Make a hole in the center of each pot top. Stick a stem into each hole. Glue in place. Let the glue dry.

10. Punch a hole in the top of each flower. Tie a piece of carpet thread through each hole.

11. Punch holes around the frame. Tie the flowers to it.

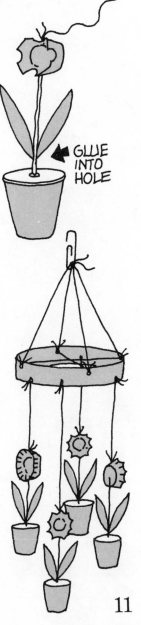

11

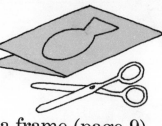

FISH

1. Make a frame (page 9).

2. Fold a piece of tissue paper in half. Draw fish on it. Cut them out. You will have matching pairs of fish.

3. Spread glue on one side of one fish. Press cotton onto the glue.

4. Glue a piece of carpet thread to the cotton as shown. Glue on the matching fish.

5. Do the same with each pair of fish. Let the glue dry.

6. Paint the fish as you wish.

7. Punch holes around the frame. Tie the fish to it.

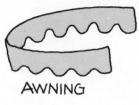

STAPLE STRAWS

AWNING

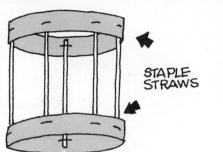

MERRY-GO-ROUND

1. Make a frame (page 9).

2. Make another oak tag circle the same size as the frame.

3. Staple straws between the circles as shown for poles.

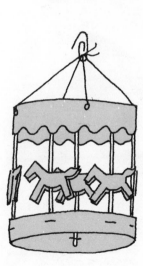

GLUE PAIR TO POLE

4. Make an awning from art paper. Glue it around the frame.

5. Fold a piece of art paper in half. Draw animals on it. Cut them out. You will have matching pairs of animals.

6. Glue matching animals to each side of each pole as shown.

13

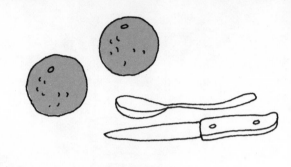

PAPER

JACK-O'-LANTERNS

1. Make a frame (page 9).

2. Slice the tops from small juice oranges.

3. Scoop the pulp out with a spoon or your fingers. Wash and dry the orange shells.

4. Stuff the shells with paper. Let them dry a couple of days.

5. Remove the paper. Paint a scary face on the outside of each shell.

HOLES

6. Punch a hole in each side of the jack-o'-lanterns as shown.

7. Cut pieces of string. Put the string through the holes to make handles.

8. Tie a piece of carpet thread to each handle.

9. Punch holes around the frame. Tie the jack-o'-lanterns to it.

WITCHES

1. Make a frame (page 9).

2. Make egg cup forms (page 8).

3. Paint the forms to look like witches' heads.

4. On art paper, draw circles the size of a coffee cup. Cut them out. Each whole circle will be the brim of a witch's hat.

5. Cut some of the circles in half. Each half will make the crown of a witch's hat.

6. Shape each half-circle into a cone as shown. Glue in place. Let the glue dry.

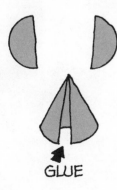

GLUE

7. To make a hat, glue a crown to one of the whole circles. Let the glue dry.

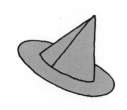

8. Cut out the center of the circle. Glue the hat to a witch's head. Let the glue dry.

CUT OUT

9. For a dress, cut a length of crepe paper. Fold it in half.

FOLD

10. Tie a piece of carpet thread around the paper near the fold. This will be the neck of the dress.

11. For arms, cut a shorter length of crepe paper. Tie a piece of carpet thread near each end.

MORE ➡

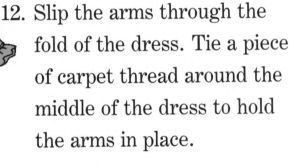

12. Slip the arms through the fold of the dress. Tie a piece of carpet thread around the middle of the dress to hold the arms in place.

13. Glue the neck of the dress to a witch's head. Let the glue dry.

14. Punch a hole in the top of the hat. Tie a piece of carpet thread through the hole.

15. Punch holes around the frame. Tie the witches to it.

18

SKELETONS AND GHOSTS

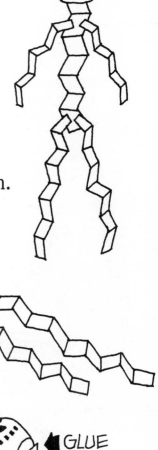

1. Make a frame (page 9).

2. Make egg cup forms (page 8).

3. Paint the forms to look like skeleton or ghost heads.

4. For each skeleton, cut strips of paper for the arms, legs and body. Fold them as shown.

5. Glue arms and legs to a body. Let the glue dry.

6. Glue a body to each skeleton head. Let the glue dry.

GLUE

MORE

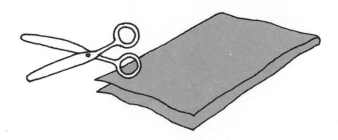

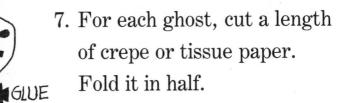

7. For each ghost, cut a length of crepe or tissue paper. Fold it in half.

8. Tie a piece of carpet thread around the paper near the fold. This will be the ghost's neck.

9. Glue a neck to each ghost head. Let the glue dry.

PIPE
CLEANER

10. Make a small hole in the top of each head.

11. Tie a piece of carpet thread to a piece of pipe cleaner for each figure.

12. Stick a pipe cleaner through the hole in each head.

13. Punch holes around the frame. Tie the figures to it.

TURKEYS

1. Make a frame (page 9).

2. Make egg cup forms (page 8).

3. On art paper, draw circles the size of a saucer. Cut them out.

4. Cut each circle into quarters. Glue a quarter-circle to each form for a turkey's tail.

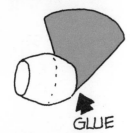

GLUE

5. Cut pipe cleaners in half. These will be the turkeys' legs and necks.

6. Make holes in each form for the legs and neck. Stick a pipe cleaner into each hole. Glue them in place. Let the glue dry.

7. Bend the bottom of each leg to make a foot.

8. Bend the end of each neck to make a head.

9. Paint the turkeys. Let the paint dry.

10. Tie a piece of carpet thread to a piece of pipe cleaner for each turkey.

11. Make a hole in the center of the back of each turkey. Stick a pipe cleaner through each hole.

12. Punch holes around the frame. Tie the turkeys to it.

CHRISTMAS STOCKINGS

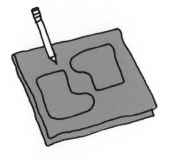

1. Make a frame (page 9).

2. Fold art or tissue paper in half. Draw stocking shapes on it. Cut them out. You will have matching pairs of shapes.

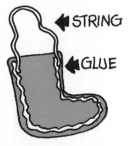

STRING

GLUE

3. For each stocking, put glue around the edges of one side of one shape. Do not put glue across the top.

4. Cut a piece of string. Put the ends in the glue as shown to make a handle.

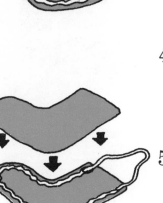

5. Press the matching shape over the glue. Let the glue dry.

6. Tie a piece of carpet thread to each handle.

7. Punch holes around the frame. Tie the stockings to it.

8. For candy canes, paint stripes around pipe cleaners. Let the paint dry.

9. Bend one end of each pipe cleaner to make a cane. Put the canes in the stockings.

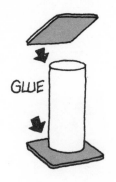

GLUE

CANDLES

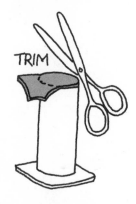

TRIM

1. Make a frame (page 9).

2. Glue pieces of cardboard to each end of toilet tissue tubes. Let the glue dry.

3. Cut the cardboard to fit.

4. Paint these candles as you wish. Let the paint dry.

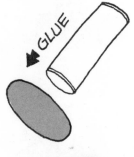

GLUE

5. For candle holders, glue a larger circle of art paper to the bottom of each candle.

6. Make a hole in the center of the top of each candle.

HOLE

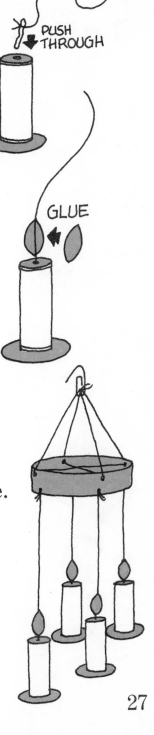

7. For each candle, tie a piece of carpet thread to a piece of pipe cleaner.

8. Stick a pipe cleaner through each hole.

9. For flames, cut pieces of art or crepe paper as shown. Glue a piece to each side of the thread at the top of the candle.

10. Punch holes around the frame. Tie the candles to it.

27

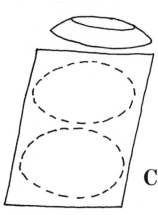

CHRISTMAS TREES

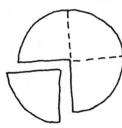

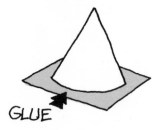

1. Make a frame (page 9).

2. On art paper, draw circles the size of saucers. Cut them out.

3. Cut away about one fourth of each circle as shown.

4. Shape the rest of the circle into a cone. Glue in place. Let the glue dry.

5. For each tree, glue the bottom of a cone to a piece of art paper. Let the glue dry. Then cut the paper to fit.

GLUE

GLUE

6. For tree trunks, paint paper drinking straws.

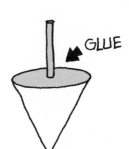

7. Make a hole in the bottom of each cone. Stick a trunk into each hole. Glue in place. Let the glue dry.

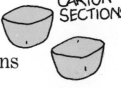

8. For tree stands, cut the sections of an egg carton apart. Trim the tops of the egg cups to make them even.

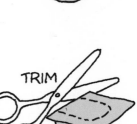

9. Glue a piece of art paper to the top of each egg cup. Let the glue dry. Trim the paper to fit.

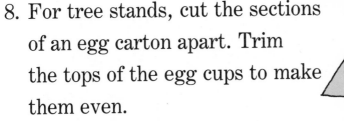

10. Paint the stands. Let the paint dry.

MORE ▶

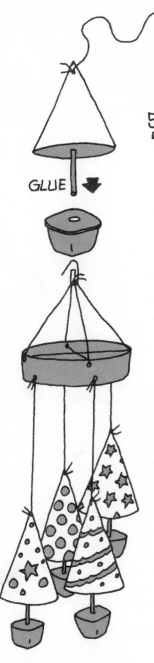

GLUE

11. Make a hole in the center of the top of each stand. Stick a trunk into each hole. Glue in place. Let the glue dry.

12. Decorate the trees as you wish.

13. Punch a hole through the top of each tree. Tie a piece of carpet thread through each hole.

14. Punch holes around the frame. Tie the trees to it.

CURLY QUES

1. Make a frame (page 9).

2. On art paper, draw circles the size of a coffee cup. Cut them out.

3. Start at the edge of each circle. Cut around and around as shown.

4. Punch a hole through the center of each circle. Tie a piece of carpet thread through each hole.

5. Punch holes around the frame. Tie the curly ques to it.

31

YARN JUMBLES

1. Make a frame (page 9).

2. Soak different-colored pieces of yarn in liquid starch.

3. Blow up several small balloons. Tie the tops.

4. Wind the wet yarn around the balloons.

WET YARN

5. When the yarn is dry, pop the balloons and carefully take them out.

6. Tie a piece of carpet thread to the yarn at the top of each jumble.

7. Punch holes around the frame. Tie the jumbles to it.

SNOWMEN

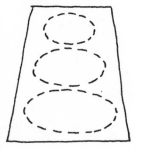

1. Make a frame (page 9).

2. On paper, draw three circles of different sizes. Cut them out.

3. Place the circles as shown. Draw around them. Cut out the shape. This is your pattern.

4. On cardboard, use your pattern to draw snowmen. Cut them out.

CARDBOARD

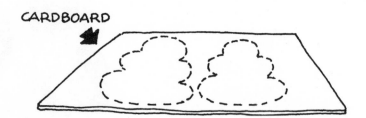

5. Punch a hole in the top of the head of each snowman. Tie a piece of carpet thread through each hole.

GLUE

COTTON

6. Spread glue on one side of a snowman. Press cotton onto the glue. Do this for each one.

7. Turn the snowmen over and do the same on the other sides.

8. Dip the tip of a paintbrush in paint. Dot eyes, nose, mouth and buttons on each snowman.

9. Punch holes around the frame. Tie the snowmen to it.

HEARTS

1. Make a frame (page 9).

2. Fold art paper in half. Draw hearts on it. Cut them out. You will have matching pairs of hearts.

3. Cut long pieces of carpet thread.

4. Put glue along the center of a heart. Lay a piece of carpet thread on the glue.

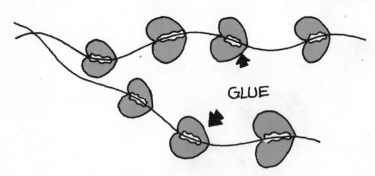

GLUE

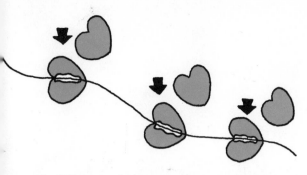

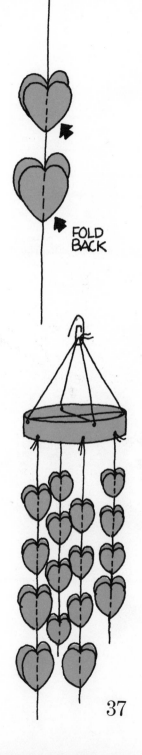

FOLD BACK

5. Place the matching heart on top of the thread.

6. Continue to glue hearts along the thread until it is full.

7. Do the same for each thread. Let the glue dry.

8. Fold each heart back from the center as shown.

9. Punch holes around the frame. Tie the hearts to it.

BASKETS

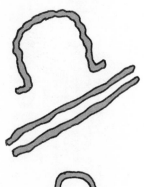

1. Make a frame (page 9).

2. Cut the sections of an egg carton apart. Trim the tops of the egg cups to make them even.

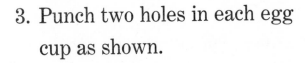

3. Punch two holes in each egg cup as shown.

4. Cut some pipe cleaners in half. Shape each piece into a handle.

5. Stick the ends of a handle through the holes in an egg cup. Bend the ends to hold them in place. Do the same for each cup.

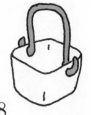

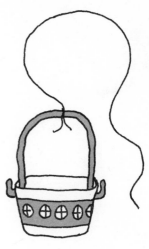

6. Paint and decorate the baskets
   if you wish.

7. Tie a piece of carpet thread
   to the center of each handle.

8. Punch holes around the frame.
   Tie the baskets to it.

9. Fill the baskets with small
   candies, nuts or raisins.

BUNNIES

1. Make a frame (page 9).

2. Make egg cup forms (page 8).

3. Paint the forms to look like bunny heads.

4. Cut bunny ears out of art paper.

5. Glue ears to each head.

6. Glue or paint on whiskers.

7. Cut a short piece of carpet
   thread for each bunny.
   Tie a piece of pipe cleaner
   to one end.

8. Make a small hole in the
   top of a bunny head. Stick
   the pipe cleaner through
   the hole.

9. Punch holes around the
   frame. Tie the bunnies
   to it.

MAY POLE

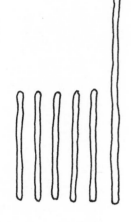

1. Make a frame (page 9).

2. For each figure, you will need one whole pipe cleaner and five halves.

3. Bend the whole pipe cleaner into an oval shape for the body. Twist the ends in place.

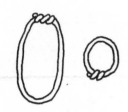

4. Bend one half pipe cleaner into an oval shape for the head. Twist the ends in place.

GLUE

5. Twist pipe-cleaner halves around the body for arms and legs. Put glue around the twists. Then put the head in place and glue it to the body. Let the glue dry.

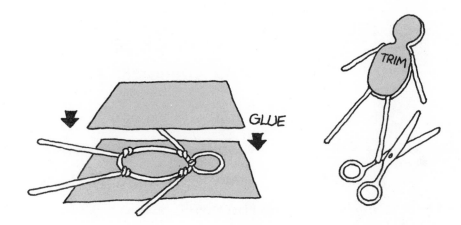

6. Glue paper on both sides of the head and body. Let the glue dry. Trim the paper to fit.

7. Paint the figures as you wish.

8. Cut out and glue crepe paper clothes to the figures as shown.

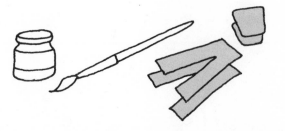

MORE

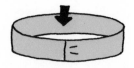

9. Make an oak tag circle the same size as the frame.

STAPLE LEGS

10. Bend the legs of the figures to look as if they are walking. Staple the legs to the circle.

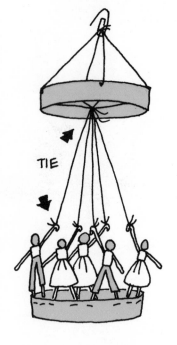

TIE

11. Cut a piece of yarn for each figure. Tie one end of each piece of yarn to the center strings of the frame.

12. Bend the end of one arm of each figure to make a hook. Tie the other end of each piece of yarn around one of the hooks.

MONKEYS

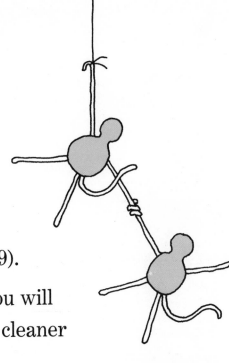

1. Make a frame (page 9).

2. For each monkey, you will
   need one whole pipe cleaner
   and six halves.

3. Follow steps three through
   six on pages 42 and 43.

GLUE

4. Twist a pipe-cleaner half
   around the bottom of the body
   between the legs for a tail.
   Put glue on the twist.

MORE ➡

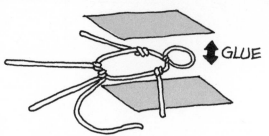

GLUE

TRIM

5. Glue paper on both sides of the head and body. Let the glue dry. Trim the paper to fit.

6. Paint the monkeys as you wish.

7. Punch holes around the frame.

8. Tie a short piece of carpet thread through each hole.

9. Tie each thread to an arm, leg or tail of a monkey.

10. Join other monkeys to these by twisting arms, legs or tails to each other.

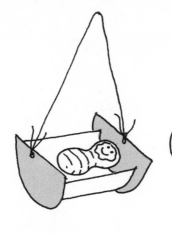

CRADLES

1. Make a frame (page 9).

2. Cut toilet tissue tubes in half. Then cut each half into two parts as shown for cradle beds.

3. On art paper, draw circles the size of a small glass. Cut out the circles.

4. Cut each circle in half. Glue a half-circle to each end of the cradle beds as shown to make rockers.

5. Paint the cradles if you wish.

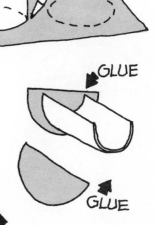

MORE ➡

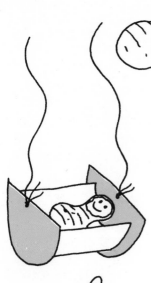

6. Paint peanuts to look like babies wrapped in blankets. Let the paint dry.

7. Glue a baby into each cradle.

8. Punch a hole through the center of each end of the cradles. Tie a piece of carpet thread through each hole.

9. Punch holes around the frame. Tie the cradles to it.

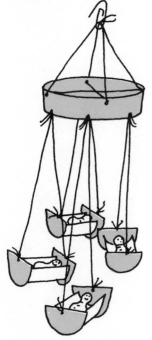

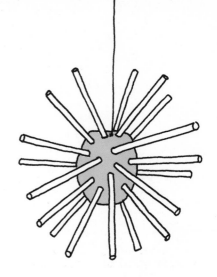

STRAW BURSTS

1. Make a frame (page 9).

2. Make egg cup forms (page 8).

3. Paint the forms if you wish.

4. Make holes all over each form.

5. Tie a piece of carpet thread to a piece of pipe cleaner for each form.

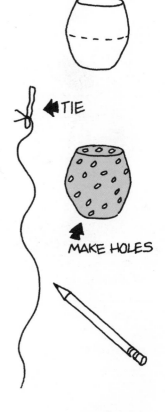

TIE

MAKE HOLES

MORE

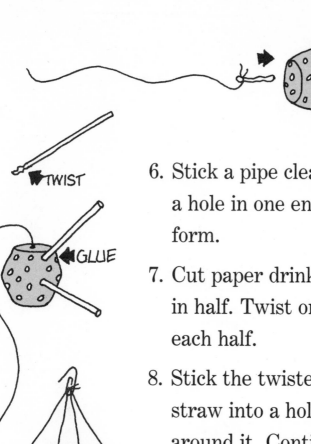

6. Stick a pipe cleaner through a hole in one end of each form.

7. Cut paper drinking straws in half. Twist one end of each half.

8. Stick the twisted end of a straw into a hole. Put glue around it. Continue doing this until all the holes are filled.

9. Punch holes around the frame. Tie the straw bursts to it.

CLOWNS

1. Make a frame (page 9).

2. Make egg cup forms (page 8).

3. Paint the forms to look like clown heads.

4. On art paper, draw circles the size of a coffee cup. Cut them out.

5. Cut each circle in half. Shape each half into a cone as shown to make a clown's hat. Glue in place. Let the glue dry.

 GLUE

MORE ➡

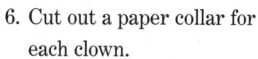

GLUE

6. Cut out a paper collar for each clown.

7. Glue a hat and a collar to each clown's head. Let the glue dry.

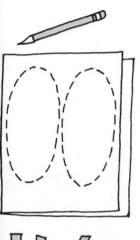

8. Fold pieces of art paper. Cut out clown body shapes as shown. You will have matching pairs of shapes.

9. Cut strips of paper for arms and legs. Fold as shown.

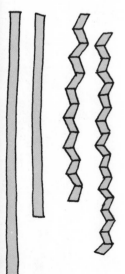

10. Glue arms and legs to one of each pair of body shapes. Then glue on the matching shape, leaving a small piece at the top unglued.

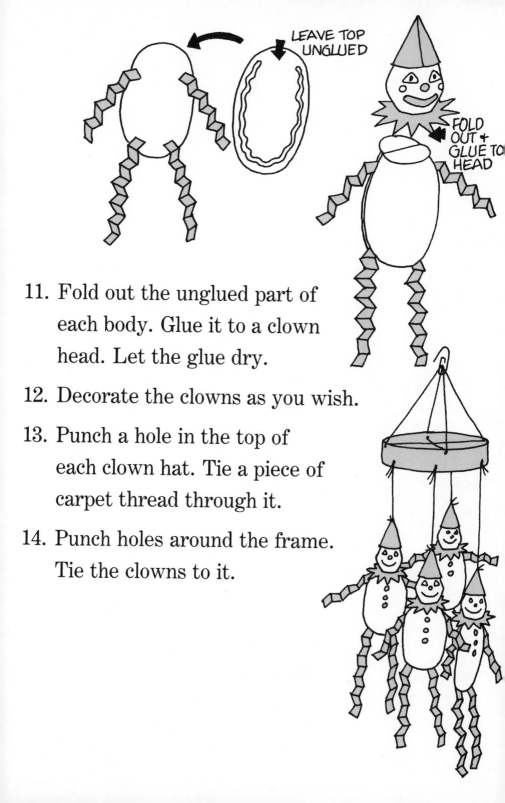

11. Fold out the unglued part of each body. Glue it to a clown head. Let the glue dry.

12. Decorate the clowns as you wish.

13. Punch a hole in the top of each clown hat. Tie a piece of carpet thread through it.

14. Punch holes around the frame. Tie the clowns to it.

PUNCH HOLES

BUGS

GLUE

TRIM

1. Make a frame (page 9).

2. Cut the sections of an egg carton apart. Trim the tops of the egg cups to make them even.

3. Punch holes around each egg cup where legs and eyes will go.

4. Glue the bottom of each egg cup to a piece of paper. Trim the paper to fit.

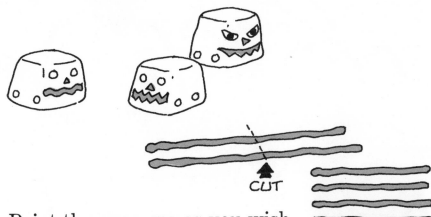

5. Paint the egg cups as you wish.

6. For legs, cut some pipe cleaners in half. Paint them. Let the paint dry.

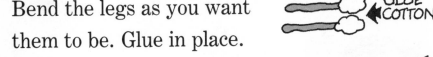

7. Stick one into each leg hole. Bend the legs as you want them to be. Glue in place.

GLUE COTTON

8. For eyes, cut some pipe cleaners into fourths. Glue cotton around one end of each.

9. Dip the cotton into paint. Let the paint dry.

PAINT

MORE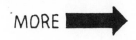

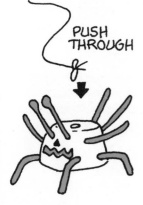

PUSH
THROUGH

GLUE

10. Stick the ends of the pipe
cleaners into the eye holes.
Glue in place.

11. Add horns, feelers or
anything else you want.

12. Tie a piece of carpet thread
to a piece of pipe cleaner
for each bug.

13. Make a hole in the center
of the back of each bug.
Stick the pipe cleaners
through the holes.

14. Punch holes around the frame.
Tie the bugs to it.

POPCORN

1. Make a frame (page 9).

2. Thread a needle with a long piece of thread.

3. String popcorn on the thread. Leave enough thread at each end to tie to the frame.

4. Make as many strings of popcorn as you wish.

5. To color the popcorn, mix food coloring with water. Use a paintbrush to dot color on the popcorn.

6. Punch holes around the frame. Tie each end of each string through a hole.

PICTURES

1. Make a frame (page 9).

2. Choose small pictures you want to use.

3. Fold pieces of art paper. Cut out shapes a little larger than the pictures. You will have matching pairs of each shape.

4. Cut long pieces of string.

FOLD

CUT SHAPES

GLUE

5. Put glue down the center of a shape. Lay a piece of string on the glue. Glue the matching shape on top of the string.

6. Continue to glue shapes along the string until it is filled.

7. Glue a picture on each side of each shape. Let the glue dry.

8. Punch holes around the frame. Tie the pictures to it.

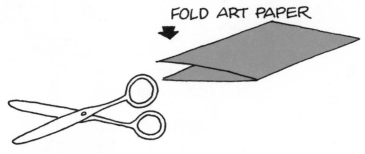

FOLD ART PAPER

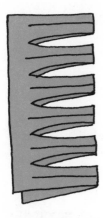

LANTERNS

1. Make a frame (page 9).

2. For each lantern, you will need a half-sheet of art paper.

3. Fold each piece of paper in half. Start at the fold and cut slits almost to the edge as shown.

4. Unfold. Glue the ends together

GLUE ENDS TOGETHER

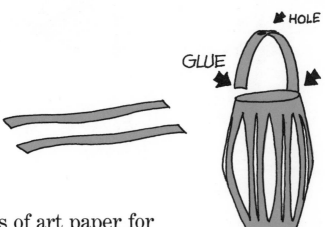

5. Cut strips of art paper for handles. Glue or staple a handle to each lantern.

6. Punch a hole in the center of each handle. Tie a piece of carpet thread through each hole.

7. Punch holes around the frame. Tie the lanterns to it.

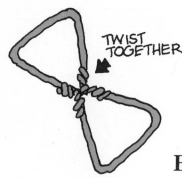

BUTTERFLIES

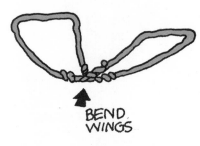

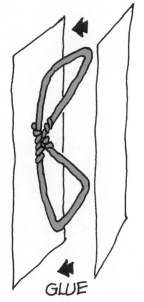

1. Make a frame (page 9).

2. Shape pipe cleaners to look like butterfly wings.

3. Twist two shapes together to make each pair of wings. Bend the wings to look as if they are flying.

4. Glue a piece of tissue paper to each side of each wing. Let the glue dry. Then trim the paper to fit.

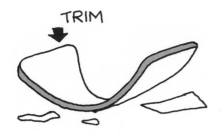

TRIM

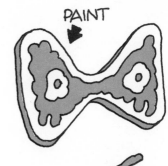

PAINT

5. Paint the wings as you wish.

6. For butterfly bodies, cut some pipe cleaners into thirds. Paint them. Let the paint dry.

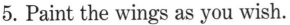

CUT + PAINT

7. Glue a body to each pair of wings.

GLUE

8. Punch a hole at the top of each wing.

9. Cut a piece of carpet thread for each butterfly. Put the thread through each wing hole as shown.

10. Punch holes around the frame. Tie the butterflies to it.

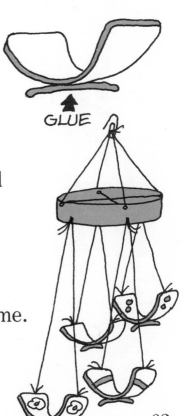

63